*The*
# Morning Glory Airport

*and Other Flights of Fancy*

# *The* Morning Glory Airport
### *and Other Flights of Fancy*

## Nancy Corbett

Book Design & Production:
Columbus Publishing Lab
www.ColumbusPublishingLab.com

Copyright © 2022 by
Nancy Corbett
LCCN: 2022915443

All rights reserved.
This book, or parts thereof, may not be
reproduced in any form without permission.

Paperback ISBN: 978-1-63337-658-8
E-Book ISBN: 978-1-63337-659-5

Printed in the United States of America
1 3 5 7 9 10 8 6 4 2

*For Bob…*

*Man of God, faithful husband, cheerful greeter at the church door, diligent employer and craftsman, beloved companion.*

*Thank you for encouraging me to write…
and to publish.*

# Good Morning Glory

In early spring
I committed
your last year's seeds
to the warming soil.
I had kept them sacred
from winter's rages,
lying wrapped, yet seeable,
on the shelf where
my prized books live.

And when the time was right. . .
you began your rebirth.

Now in mid-June
your lush leaves creep
quietly up the
crossed wire fence.

## NANCY CORBETT

How secretive you are
with your growing miracle
climbing heavenward

Like me.

Soon your beautiful, blue, bugle blossoms
will call me to a new day.

Truly, joy comes in the morning,
Glory!

# Introduction

It all began in sixth grade. Miss Smith, our teacher and the reigning principal at the time, commented to my mother that she thought my project involving paper birds on a fence was "creatively artistic." I was off and running. It's amazing what praise can do! The running was seemingly at a slow pace because here it is more than a half century later and I'm just getting around to another creative endeavor about birds. This time I've been watching the birds in my back yard, feeding them faithfully, and marveling at their magnificent variety. Of course, I consider them from the view point of a retired English teacher, not a science buff. I did buy a copy of *National Geographic Backyard Guide to the Birds of North America (second edition) by Jonathan Alderfer and Noah Strycker* and tried to be a little authentic in my bird descriptions. But they are not Gospel truths. The only one I *know* is "Look at the birds of the air; they do not sow or reap or store away in barns, and yet your heavenly Father feeds them. Are you not much more valuable than they?" (Matthew 6:26 NIV)

Several years ago my morning glories were profuse. They covered the six sections of chain link fence along one side of the enclosure where our dogs Emily and Charlotte can run free. They were aflutter with purple, pink, blue, and white as well as mixed variations of the color scheme. I watched as the birds flew into the foliage, paused, then moved on to the feeders. ***It was like an airport!***

Four full feeders attracted most of the birds, but there were two tubular Finch feeders as well. I began to think of them as the Thistle Restaurant. It was great fun to imagine what these airborne friends might be thinking. So here are some possibilities. You may think of others. I tried to check if they might be found in Southeastern Ohio, but perhaps relied on poetic license to include some aliens.

Once I got involved with the *Morning Glory Airport*, I realized that I had written a number of other pieces about nature or memorable pets. How could I include them? Why not consider them as other "flights of fancy"? So you will meet Ray Racoon, Ferguson Frog, Mary Catherine Orangespot, Willie, and others.

At this stage of life, I wonder why it seems important to me to publish things I think about.

Other people often think the same thoughts…or even more profound ones. I've determined that my purpose in writing is simply to leave a marker (other than a tombstone) that I lived here on Earth, enjoying God's creation with awe and appreciation.

Nancy Corbett
Spring, 2022

# Cardinals

Cardinals move to their priestly posts,
On pilgrimage to be fed.
Their stately robes of crimson
Are the finest shades of red.

They dine at The Holy Feeder,
And here's one thing I'm guessing:
Before they eat, each Cardinal
Says his mealtime blessing.

Back from lunch, in a green-leaf pulpit.
They preach a message fine:
"Only a gloriously joyful God
Could make Nature so divine."

So why are they here in Back Yard?
They're to bless the planting of seed.
Morning glories really love their prayers
And feel blessing is what they need.

Soon the sprouts will peak above the soil
On the fence they'll intertwine.
A breath-taking moment; Thank you, God.
For this glance at your work divine.

# Mrs. Robin
## Dedicated Mother and Public Relations Executive

She busily hops about on her way
through the airport now.
Previously promoting spring was
her PR company's goal.

Meanwhile, she found materials
to nest in for egg-laying.
She must not get maternity leave
because she poured over her paperwork
as she sat atop the nest—waiting.

Before long, little blue baby bird
containers broke open and
it was truly SPRING.

She busily filled demanding, open beaks
With worm spaghetti.

## NANCY CORBETT

She continued to keep the nest secure and soon
her fledglings
took off full-feathered and
ready to fly on their own.

Mama Robin/PR Exec
Two jobs well done.

# Bluebirds

The bluebird of happiness…
hasn't appeared.

His flight plan hasn't apparently
been cleared.

Perhaps he's just too busy to travel,
fearful his happiness might unravel.

Other passengers can be unruly
but the bluebird has a secret, truly…

"*Choose* to be happy—and be content.
don't miss out on joy, for life's quickly spent."

# Bluejays

Members of the Blue Jay Team
Are easily seen arriving
Tough and lively, also smart;
They sometimes seem conniving.

You ask the sport these fellows play?
The question is absurd!
It's basketball; you should have guessed.
Star player? LARRY BIRD.

# Chickadees

Rah, Rah, Rah, -- Sis, Boom, Bah.
The Chickadees come through the gate.
They're ready to cheer for the Blue Jays,
And simply don't want to wait.

Their vigor never lessens…
If the team is winning or not.
Their routines are polished and lively.
Other cheer crews would say they're "hot".

I thought Chickadees were quiet;
But hearing them cheer, is it odd?
Such cute little birds have worked to become

A boisterously happy squad.

Yay, Blue Jays!

# Finches

I love to watch the Finches come.
They're sunlight on the wing.
They flutter to the feeder
And speak perpetual spring.

They seem aloof from others
At the Thistle Restaurant
These darlings share their business lunch
Each looks a debutante.

Their coats of sparkling yellow
Are in fashion—it's a cinch.
The company they represent?
Of course- Abercrombie and Finch.

# Sparrows

Here come the Sparrows—each in speckled vest,
All are preparing to do their best.
They have a performance soon in Back Yard.
So clearing the airport isn't hard.

It's Gospel music they'll be singing
A hearty enthusiasm they'll be bringing.
In fact, you should know it's very liable
Their songs will tell you they're in the Bible.

They sing with JOY, no hint of despair.
They remind their listeners, they're in God's care!

"Look at the birds of the air; they do not sow or reap or store away in barns, and yet your heavenly Father feeds them. Are you not much more valuable than they?"
Matthew 6:26 NIV

# Hummingbirds

Hummingbird visits are often fleeting.
Perhaps they're on their way to a meeting
Of back-up singers, who hummmmmm the tune
As starring warblers chirp and croon.

Still, they pause for a crimson treat
While they keep humming the back-up beat.
Thanks for the joy in your hovering and humming.
You've made my day just by coming.

# Mourning Doves

The Mourning Doves weep
In sets of two.
They pause in the airport
As they're coming through.

I wonder if they have a
Funeral to attend
Or they're off to visit
And ailing friend.

Whatever their goal—
No need to wait.
Everything's better when
They're with their mate.

# Gwen Wren

Gwen Wren needs a place of her own.
She's at the airport gate.
She carries a tape measure, magazines, and such
And ponders her interest rate.

Fact is, she's <u>very</u> interested
In getting a tiny house.
She's planning to start a family
(She and her little spouse).

The Realtor Birds are waiting for her.
The papers are ready to sign,
Her Back Yard home is move-in ready
And surely will work out fine.

Gwen is thrilled with the prospect of her new home.
It may seem somewhat incidental,
But Gwen had really been worried
She'd have to live in a wren-tal.

# Nuthatch

"There's one in every crowd," they say.
The "class clown" or "life of the party."
No one needs to encourage this guy
With his spunk and zip, quite hearty.

He's one we call the "Nuthatch."
He should get help, I assert,
With his therapist taking notes as he talks,
Discovering his hidden hurt.

What does a nuthatch have to share?
Does he have a hectic life?
Does he have a lot of children?
Or a mean, contentious wife?

## NANCY CORBETT

I wish you luck, Mr. Nuthatch.
I hope your appointment goes well.
But privacy rules prevent me
From sharing the stories you tell.

Just know that the rest of us sometimes
Grin and joke when we're angry or sad.
You're actually probably "normal,"
Not "crazy" or "whack-o" or "bad!"

You're not "evil" or "vicious" or "wild;"
You are not a "worthless slouch."
Your best bet, and here's good advice…
Take a nap on the therapist's couch!

# Swallows

Deep in the dark green foliage
The swallows gather to talk
Their voices are soft and mellow
With nary a squeak or a squawk.

They're just back from Capistrano
Where they went to the Swallow Convention
And learned from thoracic surgeons
Some important advice to mention.

The doctors urge patients…"Don't smoke; it's bad
For your throat--smoking can cause cancer;
But if the patient simply has a sore throat
Here is the problem's answer:

Rest, drink fluids, take Vitamin "C"
Heed our friendly warning
Gargle warm salt water, take two aspirin
And call us in the morning."

# Woodpeckers

A construction(?) crew is coming through,
But it is my intuition
That the Woodpecker Company
Is better at demolition.

I suspect it's Morse code they use
As they tap and tap and tap.
I haven't studied enough to know
If, instead, they're seeking sap.

They're probably messaging each other
"Hey, here's a delicious tree.
Come over, we'll drill together"
But that's probably not to be.

They're beautiful with their red top knot.
Their work ethic is very good.
They set a lively example,
Then fly off to the nearby wood.

# Mafia Birds

Strutting around the airport
A very large presence indeed,
Are the Mafia Birds (the Black Birds),
A group we really don't need.

In their hugeness, they scare little travelers
They steal all the feed on the ground.
Others avoid the airport
When the Mafia Birds are around.

In his dark overcoat and fedora
Uncle Guido hunts knee caps to break.
Luigi offers assistance.
How many of them does it take?

# NANCY CORBETT

Meanwhile, I watch and I wonder
If birds really do have knees
But these ruthless criminals have their way
And exhort from whomever they please.

I laugh at their crazy appearance.
It's absolutely bizarre.
Their gold watches hide in vest pockets
And they each crunch a hefty cigar.

It's a rough bunch here at the airport.
Dark overcoats harbor each goon.
Take heart, though, I've called the police birds
And they will be coming soon.

# Morning Glory Airport Closed

The Morning Glory Airport
Has closed down for repair.
But local traffic comes each day.
No need to feel despair.

I've left some vines that intertwined
Across the fence they need
To pause before they move on to
The feeders with full speed.

These feathered aviators
Are dressed in blues and reds.
Some are striped or spotted
With top knots on their heads.

What a cheery crowd they are!
They chatter and drop lunch
To waiting squirrels beneath them.
They're all a happy bunch.

# NANCY CORBETT

Come spring. …
The crowd will welcome a different kind of seed!

I'll plant my morning glory seeds.
The fence-top will spring forth.
More vari-colored flyers
Will be glad they came back north.

Tour buses will crisscross the yard
Letting viewers see the splendor:
Billions of beautiful blossoms. . .
Add a cotton candy vendor?

Hot dog stand? Perhaps balloons?
Like a circus, I'm proposing.
We'll see the airport come to life
After winter forced its closing.

Wait with me to see spring come.
You'll see. *"I'm never bored"*\*
As the Morning Glory Airport
Is gloriously restored

\*These words came from my great-aunt, when I visited her in a nursing home and naively asked, "How do you spend your time now, Aunt Goldie?" As I age, I'm also learning that boredom is a choice…as is happiness!

Illustrations for this poem were created by Linda Graham,
an artist who is a friend from church and the Ladies Bible Study.

# MORNING GLORY AIRPORT

# Other Flights of Fancy-Iris

Looking over the list of pieces included in "Other Flights of Fancy," I'm fondly remembering the circumstances that brought these stories and musings into existence.

I recall happy years at Willow Lakes, where we welcomed a number of pets like Fred, Annie and others. We thrived on the general chaos of our lives. There were outdoor feathered friends like Max, the swan, and Esther Jane Elizabeth, the wild goose. ( I forgot to tell about Iris, the heron who flew in occasionally. She was called "Iris," because she came very unexpectedly and we thought she was the flower, Iris, as she stood at the little lake's edge. After that spectacular appearance, we watched carefully for her.) Ferguson Frog came from those days too. You may wish to read about Ferguson with grandchildren so they can mimic the sounds made by the "members of the orchestra."

Although "Ray Raccoon" comes from my teaching experiences, this is another poem which is best read aloud, using a British accent, perhaps in costume as a "distinguished poet." Someday I may put together a book about those teaching days and some of my teachers who led me to become an educator.

## MORNING GLORY AIRPORT

Now that I've retired, my back yard has become a source of real joy, not only for its flowers and feeders, but also for bird-watching, using my little binoculars—hoping the neighbors don't think I'm spying on them.

This splattering of prose and poetry are in no particular order; they are simply here for your consideration and enjoyment.

# Mary Cat-herine Orange-Spot, Madonna Cat

Mary Catherine Orange-spot is a kitten of beauty and grace
And Mary Catherine Orange-spot has an "M" upon her face.
It's just above the bridge of her nose
Where usually a frowning question goes.

But Mary Catherine is quite content in her lovely kitten ways.
She lies in the sun when the day has begun and basks in its warming rays.
And while she purrs, she dreams of her kin who also bore the "M."
Her song rises and falls as she recalls the legend surrounding them.

Long ago in Bethlehem on a night that had been quite strange
An event occurred in a stable small that caused the world to change.
A man and a woman, so very tired, had had nowhere else to go.
"No room," the innkeeper said. "There's not one bed," and so
Their only choice was to come to sleep surrounded by noisy cattle and sheep.

The smell was bad, the light was poor, a breeze blew in around the door,
But Mary and Joseph could travel no more; their spirits were worn and their feet were sore.
So there they stayed for the night. But soon there came a brilliant light.
And in the star-beam an amazing sight; the animals shook their heads left and right…

A baby was being born!!! The drama began to unfold
And so the story is told, since the night was quite cold,
The cows got closer and offered their breath to warm the Bethlehem air.
The other livestock lent their warmth as the infant was wrapped with care.

Soft swaddling cloths were wound around him; hardly a sound was made.
The stable creatures gathered close. In a manger He was laid.
And while the baby was cradled in straw, a stable kitten, with tender paw
Jumped into the manger and sat in awe…as the baby began to weep.
She patted the baby and purred a song to put the infant to sleep.
Mary, who longed for the baby to rest, reached out with a sense of relief.

There on the kitten's forehead, the Madonna touched the fur
And forever the kitten's offspring would show that touch from her.
That gesture of love from the Christ child's mother left an "M" as a permanent mark.
Mary was pleased that the kitten could sing in surroundings cold and stark.
The kitten snuggled up close to the child and purred as Mary softly smiled.
The warmth and the music kept all beguiled, even the animals, tame and wild.
They must have known God's love was shown by the gift He gave that night.
That infant small later died for us all to give us life and light.

The kitten knew that it was true Christ's coming to earth was a miracle.
She welcomed Him in the stable dim with her song so soft and lyrical.
It's a beautiful thing to sing for a king, but to sing for the King of Kings:
Measure for measure,
This moment to treasure,
Brought the kind of pleasure
That "serving" Him always brings.

Today, as I sat, Mary Catherine, our cat, who has the "M" on her face,
Spoke to me of God's love so free and His far-reaching grace.
Across the distance of time and space, His love redeems the human race!
There is hope and love to spare. … We have that message to share.

Mary Catherine's spot is color she's got; above her heart it lies.
She wears it like a medallion, as if an Olympic prize.
I'd give her a medal myself, for opening my eyes.
That spot on her heart looks very smart;
In fact, Mary Catherine's a work of art.
Her forehead gem, that mark of "M," is just a <u>legend</u> to tell.
But seeing it brought to me a thought on which I want to dwell:

If <u>God</u> were doing the marking with an "M" on me as a sign
I would know the "M" would show He's saying "You are MINE!"
I'm so glad for this happy moment, when my heart and mind are stirring.
My song?  I belong—to the King—and I feel like purring!

# A Tale of Two Sisters

Emily Beagle and Charlotte Sharpei
Lived at the shelter..until one day
Along came a man with a heart for a pup.
So Emily Beagle jumped down and up.

The man was still sad--for his dog of long years
Had gone to dog heaven; he was in tears.
Dear Annie, in heaven, had had a long life.
"No more dogs!" said the man and his wife.

Em smiled with her bright eyes, a grin on her face.
Maybe he'd take her away from this place.
The keepers were kind, no cause to complain.
Warm in their shelter, she was out of the rain.

She had enough food, a nice pat then and now.
Still, Emily wanted a home of her own somehow.
But there was Charlotte; her sister, for real.
Was there hope the man wanted <u>two</u> dogs in the deal?

Charlotte was not so pretty as Em.
She would have wrinkles. Would the man like them?
Her fur was bristly and she was all dark.
She had black eyes too, and a shrill little bark.

Yes, the man nodded.  He'd take Emily.
But he'd planned for <u>one</u> dog—That's the way it would be.
The man signed the papers and wanted to know
When Emily would be ready to go.

When he went home to tell of his find,
A brown, bouncy Beagle, just the right kind,
He mentioned the dark dog, sister of Em.
His wife sighed, "How could we ever separate them?"

So back to the shelter, the two went in haste.
Both knew there was actually no time to waste.
What if someone else had adopted Em's sister?
Ah, there she was!  They hugged her and kissed her.

Now Emily Beagle and Charlotte Sharpei
Live with the couple and tumble and play.
Good food and water and squeak toys galore,
Chew bones and old socks are strewn on the floor.

# MORNING GLORY AIRPORT

The dogs romp and play in the yard by the tree.
They're happy and healthy, it's plain to see.
In the mornings they help the man read the paper.
But soon they're off on another wild cape

Em finds adventure in the littlest noise.
Charlotte wants to own <u>all</u> of the toys.
Em chases Jack, the cat, with great zest.
Charlotte puts Puffie, the cat, to the test.

With four pets around… for everyone's sake…
The whole family has adjustments to make.
But it's well worth the effort to welcome the two.
Two puppies? It was the right thing to do!

In a rocker, the lady, both pups on her lap,
Settles contentedly to take a nice nap
In this house full of puppies and cats…and laughter,
All will live happily ever after.

December, 2007

*This poem became a book itself, illustrated by an artistic student (Brittany Gillespie Richard) from my speech class from Philo High School. It was also called *A Tale of Two Sisters*.

# Ferguson Frog

Ferguson Frog was a fabulous frog.
He lived at West Willow in an old hollow log.

But he did his work at the rim of the lake
Using a wonderful sound he could make.

"Glunk,"Glunk," he'd begin with his deep bass voice
Taking the melody, the song was his choice.

For Ferg was conductor of the "West Willow Creatures,"
A musical group with a number of features.

Ferguson's family kept the melody strong
With resonant tones at the base of each song.

Phil Frog sang his part from across the lake
Adding a tenor "glunk, glunk" he could make.

# MORNING GLORY AIRPORT

Farrah Frog brought the alto in so mellow
The whole combination made all hearts swell…Oh

West Willow music, with songs in the night
Filled the soft air with magic delight.

Katy Did played along on her leg violin
With Carolyn Cricket's "chirp, chirp" chiming in.

They were accompanied by all of their friends
For a symphonic evening of fine tonal blends.

From the night Carl Crow could sometimes be heard.
"Caw, Caw,' creaked in that cantankerous bird.

But nobody cared for there was such fun;
All sounds were welcome from anyone.

Terry the Turtle clicked his shell, entranced.
Fred Fish led his school as they splashed and danced.

(His group had to pause occasionally
For a bug might attract their attention, you see.)

Regal Max Swan swam his nightly ballet
Leaving the music for others to play

But the symphony grew with crescendo pitch
While a few night bird called, "Kersnitch, Kersnitch."

## NANCY CORBETT

Iris the Heron stood very tall,
Quietly observing the thrill of it all.

From her box seat in a tree by the lake
Sally Squirrel shared her voice: "Schrake, schrake,Shrake, shrake."

Timothy Toad observed from dry ground,
Blinking approval at each lovely sound.

Odetta Owl called out "Whoo, Whooo"
While Darla Dove added "Cooo, cooo."

To help keep the time, Bats, Beth and Barone,
Fluttered their wings for a metronone.

Sometimes their noises changed to a "whir,"
As they zoomed back and forth to keep things astir.

Chris Crane occasionally let out a "Whoop;"
Sam Snail slugged along, just watching the group.

But long about daylight—the crack of dawn,
Ferg would dip his conductor's baton.

For Ferguson Frog of West Willow fame
Had to rest for an up-coming night of the same

Grand music, majestic, a lovely caress,
A background for dreams and half wakefulness.

# MORNING GLORY AIRPORT

For now one who listened with head on the pillow
Has drifted away with the songs of West Willow.

Come to the lake; I'll give you a call
Some quiet evening -spring, summer, or fall.

Through the day Ferg might practice a croak now and then,
But his real contribution begins around ten

When his green, glowing grin calls his friends to perform
With their voices and instruments lively and warm.

Moonlight abounds and the stars are glistening.
And there's **JOY** all around in performing or listening.

# Ray Raccoon

T'was in the merry month of June
That first we met young Ray Racoon,
Who having fiercely angry grewn,,
Went to Arthur Ardvark for a boon.
"Help me, Arthur," he did croon,
"I have been wronged by Bob Baboon.

He promised me that very soon
He'd pay me for a lovely loon
I'd sold him for a pretty tune.
He says the day he now does rue-n
When first he chose to buy the loon.
For actually, she sang off tune.
His nasty comments he has strewn
Among my friends, who feel he's shewn
Ill will to me—Boo Hoon, Boo Hooon…
I'll bop him till he turns maroon!
He really is a silly goon!"

# MORNING GLORY AIRPORT

Before King Arthur could intervoon,
Ray took a giant cooking spoon
And started bopping Bob—who soon
Became quite darkly black and blu-en.
Poor Bob, who felt he had been hewn,
Slumped to the ground in heavy swoon.
He lay down by the big lagoon
And baked beneath the blazing noon,
And still was lying as the moon
Climbed to the sky that night in June.
Alas, Alack, had Bob been slewn?

Ah, ha, poor Bob was not aloon.
Beside him wimpered May Muldune
Whose fragrance of quite nice caloon
Had wakened some primeval rune
In Bob, and he was coming tooon!!!

Close by was grieving Ray Racoon
Who was ashamed of what he'd doon.
"Forgive me, Bob, boohoon, boohoon.
I'm just as guilty of wrong as you-n.
Could we be friends, our hearts attune?
I am so glad you were not slewn!!!"

Come sound bassoon!  Send up baloon!
Alas, alack, my tale is through-n.

[Dedicated to Carrie Schenkel, who coined the word "slewn" in an A.P Senior English Class skit in 1998.]

# Annie & Fred

How does it feel to come from being a vagabond to being a beloved member of a family. So were the words to Annie, another addition to our menagerie. Our six-year-old daughter and I had been traveling home from school and were at a busy thoroughfare late one afternoon when we saw a flash of creamy brown fur in the bushes near the street. We stopped to investigate, afraid the animal might get hit by a car. Soon we had the puppy in the car heading toward home. We called the animal shelter to let them know of our acquisition, in case the creature belonged to someone. We also called several businesses in the area where we first saw her. We named her Annie, like Little Orphan Annie in the storybook....but my friend tried to make us believe that this dog was a former circus performer. She seemed to dance on her hind legs when we attempted to pet her. She looked like the dog Benji in a movie that was popular at that time. Maybe she had been a clown who danced.

However, things got even better when Fred, the golden-red cocker spaniel, wandered into the yard one fine day. A neighbor worked at the animal shelter so she just came over to our house to check out this latest hobo. Fred smiled a somewhat toothless smile and she suggested that we just do the paperwork there at home so Fred wouldn't have to actually spend time caged up at the shelter. He seemed such a free spirit, so with a grin and a slobber, he became our dog. We had named him Fred because he had responded to that name when we tried a number of possibilities. Thinking back, perhaps someone had called him "Red" because of his coloring, but he seemed content with the name and with belonging to us.

Fred was afraid of storms even when we wrapped him lovingly in a blanket and held him as the thunder raged. It wasn't quite enough; but, of course, the storm passed. One morning Fred was shaking and we had no storm! That was the day that our City Fathers had contracted to have a local bridge demolished. We didn't feel it, but our Fred did. He must have had seismographic experience in a previous life. Again, we wrapped and held him, but to no avail. The moment I knew, though, that Fred was pre-destined to become our dog was following my foot surgery when I was side-lined to an easy chair beside which Fred sat for hours. He was a welcome, loving companion.

The best part about these two dogs is that they became good friends. If I took one dog along in the car, I did well; but if both of them went, it was chaos when I came home if they got out to travel the neighborhood as a vaudeville team together. Even though it took time to round them up and bring home, I had to laugh at their antics. What happy, fun dogs they were.

Both Annie and Fred have gone to dog heaven now, but what a pleasure it has been to reminisce about their adopting us as their family. We loved them both very much.

# Quaint Patrick

Body of white and ring tail of yellow,
You certainly are a crazy fellow.
A cat that, when God assembled you,
Made your ears and tail of different hue.
Your ears are gold as the light shines through
And your beautiful eyes are brilliant blue.
They close so softly when I stroke your white coat
Or scratch behind ears or massage your throat.
You purr out approval and I am pleased
As you drape in sleep across my knees.

I wanted a lucky Irish cat
And thought you'd be yellow to be just that;
With a white thatched-roofed cottage surrounded by green,
Just like the pictures of Ireland I've seen.
You'd sit by the door and welcome the day
And bring good luck for us both, come what may.

## NANCY CORBETT

We'd look out for rainbows, and puff clouds, and sun.
And we would speak Gaelic and only have fun.

Oh, we're not in Ireland, but I still have you
And rainbows and laughter and skies of blue.
You will always be my pot of gold,
Even at times when you're hard to hold
As you banshee screech all through the house
In search of a ball or play toy mouse.
I named you in honor of Patrick, the saint.
He would have laughed at the yellow paint
That adorns only your tail and ears;
Oh, I guess a splash on your face appears!

He would have loved you too (Saint Patrick).
You are the best cat, I love you Quaint Patrick.

# Willie

She arrived by mail that bitter, winter day—well, sort of by mail, having been shoved into our mailbox by two errant pre-teen girls who ran from their prank when my husband charged up the drive shouting loudly about federal laws and mailboxes. When he returned to the house, he simply reported the facts to my quizzical expression: "Two girls—not from our neighborhood. . . . it was a cat they had, . . .putting it in our mailbox, but it took off across Tharps' yard and I didn't see where it went after that."

I was relieved that Bob hadn't brought the cat back and that its whereabouts were unknown. I knew he couldn't let us keep another stray. Besides three young children we had adopted a few years before, we had three cats and a dog. Our home smacked of zoo already without any additions to the menagerie. Still, there was a bit of gnawing at my conscience as I thought how cold the vagabond cat would be in the biting Ohio winter.

I needn't have worried because it wasn't outdoors any longer. Somehow when the garage door had been opened briefly that afternoon, the cat had hidden itself in a partially open bag of straw. Later I heard a wheezing meow and the bedraggled feline weakly worked her way out of the bag and climbed over piles of garage junk to say hello. She should have been fluffy with white background to large black splotches. Her eyes streamed with mucus, and large sores outlined the backs of her ears. My stomach churned to see her. I picked her up. The matted fur was deceptive; she was tiny and very needy. Our indoor cats didn't always finish their food. What would be the harm in offering her their left-overs? She was ravenous . . . but not just for food!

Bob wouldn't hear of the cat coming into the house. It was probably disease-ridden and would contaminate the other pets. Of course, he was right. All of them had been strays, but we had been able to get basic shots and care. It could stay in the garage just long enough for us to get it to the local animal shelter after the weekend. I prepared a box with some soft towels and changed the drinking water several times a day because the water kept freezing. There was cat food to share and I reasoned that at least the needy kitten was out of the howling winter. It was so hungry; it would eat whatever was put before it. Surprisingly, it was most appreciative of patting and cuddling.

Monday came and Bob was "too busy" to take the cat to the shelter. I called a friend who was active there to see if a kitten of her description had been reported missing. My friend suggested that more than likely the poor little thing would be euthanized because it was sick and there were already so many strays being brought in.

Tuesday—still too busy! Gradually the days wore on. I spent time visiting with Willie in the garage several times a day. By this time, we had named her. Her blinking sore eyes and her tiny body structure had named her Wee Willie Winkie. Since she was going to the shelter, we didn't feel we could afford the vet bills and she really wasn't going to be our cat anyway. Meanwhile, she would quickly leave her sleeping quarters to wind about my legs with mutters and croons, seeming to communicate her contentment at having her very own bag of straw. I bathed her eyes with warm water, hoping to ease her discomfort. Her desires were easily met. Her cheerful acceptance of her plight was winning her a chance to live. At last came the verdict: She could stay on indefinitely in the garage!

## More about Willie...

We didn't want her to be destroyed because she had such a positive spirit, despite her apparent abuse. I bought some medication from a nearby veterinarian and finally took her to see him. He placed her on the stainless table and began looking her over carefully. As he probed about in her mouth, I spoke: "Oh, look, some of her teeth are missing. Has she lost her baby teeth?…When do you think her regular teeth will come in?" In my rambling questions, my naivete was showing.

"Why, I don't think they will come in," he responded. This cat is probably over 12 years old! More than likely she's small because she was malnourished." I was stunned. I rushed home, cat in arms, to deliver the startling news bulletin. "Dr. Miller says Willie is over 12 years old!"

Bob responded, "Well, the poor old thing. What do you think of that? She can't stay in that cold garage any longer. Twelve years old!? I guess we'll have to bring her into the house after all." He gave consent to the adoption.

It was done!

Gradually, Willie began to act like a princess. Occasionally we even called her Princess Will, or even more elegantly, Princess Willhemina. She reigned from the easy chair. The other animals grudgingly accepted her, but they had been a bit aloof themselves so, for the most part, they didn't care that she gravitated to close companionship with the human population. Garfield, a hardened feline, simply avoided her when he wasn't hissing his discontent. Mickey, a timid male tiger with white splotches, accepted Willie as a novelty needing inspection. Eighteen-year-old Corny shared laps with her. The children longed to lug her about the house doll-fashion, but we felt she needed to rest a while from her hard life. They lavished their attentions and affections on her if she chose to lie on their laps or as she groomed herself in the center of family activities. Sometime she slept with them.

I wondered if some kind, elderly person had let the kitty out one day, only to have it lose its way or be abducted by the mailbox juvenile delinquents. In our home Willie played with Legos or other debris the children dropped to her. She trained us to hunt pieces of dry dog food she had confiscated from the dog's bowl to bat around the kitchen. We scrounged dog food from beneath the stove and searched under the refrigerator as she patiently waited. In the night we would think one of the children had awakened…only to discover Willie chasing a tub-toy around the bathroom floor. Willie's zest for life delighted us all. In fact, one by one, Willie had captured our hearts. She washed herself each day and evening right before nap and bedtime. Her tummy looked like she'd had a perm, but she hadn't been allowed to leave the house since she came to us, so it had to be natural curl. Her white tufted paws suggested some regal ancestors; her black markings resembled heavy punctuation marks over her white fluffy coat. Her bushy black tail now seemed a waving explanation mark above her back. Chunky hind quarters waddled as she followed Bob about the house—a loyal disciple to her ultimate rescuer who had kept "forgetting" to take her to the animal shelter.

She is a welcome companion lying underfoot while I am in the kitchen. I mouth sillinesses, filled with baby talk. At bedtime in cold weather, she often sleeps with Bob and me. Yes, I love Willie; in fact, our whole family loves her. The lesson she has taught us is complex, but thought-provoking. Maybe it is that somehow there will always be a way to work in one more lonely, needy creature, be it human or otherwise. It may be that those whom we at first perceive to be unattractive or too emotionally demanding can become transformed when we accept them with loving hearts. But it is hard to say if the transformation has occurred in Willie, in ourselves, or both. Whatever the miracle—our mailbox cat was a message about loving the unlovely and, serendipitously, being loved in return. Willie has become a symbol of the deep need to belong to one another, just as she needed to belong to us.

# Latest bulletin...

This September we received the "gift" of a kitten! Just what we needed. Our neighbor boarded a horse on a farm on the outskirts of Zanesville and had encountered a tiny kitten with such charisma that she felt our children "really should have this kitten." Bob likes Mary (the neighbor) so he agreed. She had feared that the kitten might get kicked by a horse and killed. That really would have been a great loss because the kitten is already deeply beloved. She (Puff) has such a loving spirit that we have had to respond with love in return. Puffie, named because she was so very tiny—one and one forth pound—when she arrived —"puffed" herself up in cat-fashion to intimidate the other pets in the house. Her efforts didn't work, but she was great fun to watch. Shortly after she came, she got terribly ill. She had a virus which was further complicated by the blood-draining fleas she had entertained and then brought with her from the horse barn. She nearly died, but with lots of veterinary care—and financial investment—she has survived. I tell you about Puff because she has been adopted by Willie. When the tiny kitten came to us, Willie immediately took over her washing and nurturing. When Puff was ill, Willie seemed puzzled and a bit lost. Since Puff has recovered, the two have been inseparable. They sleep together and Willie completes a couple of very wet washings per day on her adopted baby. Puffie sometimes attacks Willie in playful fashion and the two tumble about; we suspect there is cat-chuckling going on. Willie has a communication system of little grunts and croonings. They dine in the same spot, even though they use separate bowls. Puffie began life as a calico cat, but her fur has changed as she grows. The vet describes her as having a "merle" coat. There is silver mixed with her oranges, blacks, whites, and browns. Her face looks as if she has a mask with black circles around her eyes and a tiny orange spot on her forehead. She has an orange and white chin and lots of white whiskers. She sports one yellow-orange leg as well. Actuallly, she rather resembles a disorganized patchwork. What a cutie she is—still very little. She probably always will be small because of her poor beginning.

I seldom have time to sit down very long, but this activity is becoming more appealing because now when I pause to read a newspaper or watch a little television with the family, nearly always Willie will climb on my lap only to be followed by Puff and the two will curl up together for a snooze. It is such a relaxing time to pet their little purring bodies and sense their trust and contentment. It is sometimes hard to distinguish where one cat ends and the other begins because they become so closely intertwined. Their monetary value, including all their health care expenses, is probably far less than costs would be to simulate these peaceful moments through a stress reduction seminar. God was so very kind and wise there in the Garden when He created the animals. It's interesting to consider that man may have been an afterthought.

# Esther Jane Elizabeth

Esther Jane Elizabeth was a giant wild goose who reigned
over the little lake when we lived
on West Willow.

She saw to it that her subjects (resident ducks and an occasional swan)
maintained a sense of direction and decorum.

She was a treat to observe.

Once I saw her in the take-off
mode running down the yard, finally become airborne
like a huge feathered transport plane.
She didn't go far because she considered her responsibilities
to be very important.

We had named her
Esther—like the beautiful queen in the Bible.  She saved her people.

## NANCY CORBETT

Jane—because it just fit
Elizabeth—like England's two long-lived, regal queens.

We wonder where she is today—many years later--
and question if there is a goose heaven.

# Puff

*Neighbor cat, Jack, pictured beside Puff.*

This March morning

Puff, the calico princess cat
sat on the chair back
surveying her visual kingdom.

I had raised the blind
so she could see the
birds and squirrels
skitter about in their celebration
of the coming of day.

The quiet lake beside the house
was rimmed with green bowing pines;
a lone duck floated atop the water.
It is there I saw the miracle!
Just above the water

## NANCY CORBETT

in a phantasmic ballet
steamy white vapors
leaped and swayed
in their joy of the morning.

The breeze pushed the dancers
across the mirror lake, but…
the scene was set for reflection.

How like us—humanity—
we in our vaporous existence
are swept along by the currents,
but are compelled to
rise and dance;
we cannot contain ourselves
as the sun blesses
the new day.

I turned to see Puff's response, but
in keeping with her name, she was
off on other pursuits—
Then so was I,
remembering that
such is life,—
to be loved and valued
for its potential for joy!

What is your life?
You are a mist that appears
for a little while then vanishes.
*James 4:14*

MORNING GLORY AIRPORT

# More about Puff...

**Morning Ritual**

Even the cat has a routine!
It works for her – from what I have seen.
She waits on the counter for breakfast to show,
Guarding her food from the puppies below.
She gobbles her meal with purrings of glee;
Next washes away the cat food debris.
She moves to the corner to be near the shower
And bathes herself for what seems an hour.
She wet-paws her face with additional licking,
But seems to grasp that the clock is ticking.
All things in order on her "things to do" chart
She naps in the sun and warms my heart.


**Social Climber in the Home Office**

Patchwork cat, with dreams of tigerdom,
You climb through stacks of paper "foliage"
To sit atop the strong file cabinet perch.
You stealthily observe my endeavors
From behind the clerical chaos.
Your splash/dash coloring isn't "tiger,"
Your black mask seems more "raccoon;"
But, like me, you may pretend to be anything you wish!
I am a writer today; you are a tiger

## NANCY CORBETT

No prey--my typing fingers.
The computer mouse will not be caught.
It would be beneath you to attack the little "rodent."
Rest for your day's adventures in the jungle.
I'm glad for your company.
I am using my imagination too.
So we are "kitten-dred" spirits.

# Max

Savage swan of loneliness, MAX,
You sweep across your private lake,
waiting for the "bread drop" to come again.
(Swan shall not live by bugs alone?)

With awe at your beauty bubbling in my heart,
I crumb the bread to accommodate.
Your question mark neck raises and lowers so your
watery beak can nip up the pieces.
It flashes orange while your round, black eyes
suspect me of devious designs.

I have no recipe for "swan soup."
Far more joy than a full stomach comes from watching
you preen your white feathers after a smooth, gliding swim,
or viewing your one-legged ballet on shore.
You shake your black leather, webbed foot,

stretch your neck, ruffle your wings with filament feathers—
billowing sash-like as you twirl in your dance.
Sometimes you dip to the mirror surface; your tail wags and
you rise, majestic again.
Star of the little lake, you sneak across the grass
to the fence to beg another handout for your regal performance.

You have chased me and nipped me, exerting your supreme
command of the region.

MAXMILLION!!!!!!
How aptly named you are!

I have had a million warm, inner smiles over you, Max.

Down deep, under those neatly combed feathers
beats your lonely heart, wishing your mate still lived.
Are you bored with your lake life?

We humans are poor substitutes; but with our bread offerings
and tolerance of your droppings, we show you affection and
understanding, the best we can, because we are not swans.

Perhaps you watch us, Max, in _our_ longings for "something more."
In our silly life ballet, we preen and fluff ourselves,
Nipping and chasing--to establish _our_ territory

When what we really want is
to make friends with a spunky swan like you, MAX.

# Pondering the Prodigal

What was that noise?

I had just let Corny, our cat, out that September morning. What was he doing to be making that noise? Wasn't it enough that his fellow-feline Garfield was gone? GONE….for nearly a week. No one knew where…just GONE. All the neighbors had been watching for him; the animal shelter was alerted; but the veterinarian I'd spoken to last evening was probably right when he'd said firmly, "I'm sorry, Lady, no yellow tabby has been brought into my office as an injured stray. Your cat probably just got hit by a car and crawled off somewhere to die."

That darn cat! I had worried about him from the minute I first saw him. A student had appeared at my high school classroom door with the little mite inside her jacket, protecting him from another faculty member who was supposedly a "cat-hater." I knew I'd take Garfield home when he peaked out from the girl's jacket—frost-bitten nose first, followed by frightened eyes and frost-burned ear tips. Ohio's winter had been bitter that year.

I really had become a doting parent. The ear tips had been saved and his nose had again healed to kitten pink, but his vet visits for fighting suggested all was not well emotionally. He was so unlike the mellow 12-year old Corny I had just let out the door. But Garfield was GONE and I'd have to stop reminiscing to check out those odd noises I had heard. At his age, could Corny actually be playing with something that would make that scraping rattle?

I was stunned! There sat young Garfield with his rear right foot awkwardly stretched behind him…an animal trap still attached. His plaintiff meow made me feel like crying, too.

Snatching Garfield, careful to hold the trap as well, I rushed into the house. "Bob!" I screeched to my husband. "It's Garfield! He's HOME!"

"Great! I wonder where he's been?"

"Look at him."

"Oh, poor thing. He must have been in that trap for nearly a week, then last night's rain softened the ground enough for him to pull free. I wonder if it will hurt him any more to take the trap off now; you know, the circulation will try for those toes and they're really a mess."

"He may have blood poisoning or gangrene." Bob knelt, still in shaving cream, as he carefully removed the trap, crooning to the cat who watched stupefied; his ugly foot was full of maggots!

Hurriedly rearranging his schedule, Bob would take Garfie to Dr. Denhart as soon as the vet's office opened. The kitty curled gratefully in his lap on the way as fumes from the stench-filled, rotten foot drifted upward. Garfield stubbornly refused to ride in the box with the soft blanket that Bob had prepared for him. He wanted to cuddle. It was sad to wonder if the vet could save his foot? His leg? His life?

Our joy over the returning cat had made us want to bring out tiny robes and little jeweled rings. Perhaps we should kill the fatted mouse and invite some neighborhood cats in for a celebration if Garfield survived. We suddenly felt great empathy with the Biblical Prodigal's parents.

Word came that the cat, indeed would survive, losing only two toes.

He would limp, but he would live! I was so glad he'd had enough sense to come home. Over the healing period, I considered the prodigal cat. Was that the way it had been for the Biblical son? Had he returned to find joyful acceptance and celebration, but had he continued to limp emotionally or socially for his lifetime? Dealing with his brother's resentment would surely have needed some time on the couch. (Luckily Corny seemed glad Garfield was home, for we surely couldn't afford a cat psychiatrist.) Did the real Prodigal have lingering nightmares of his pig pen days and errant carousings? In the Bible account, wasn't the father's love enough to undo all the damages? Maybe not. Perhaps the young man had scars from pig bites and forever hated corn, but he had been able to save his life by having enough sense to go home.

    I think I can identify with both man and beast. Sometimes my stubborn desires cause me to stray from God into foreign realms or deeds. I know I can expect forgiving acceptance from my Heavenly Parent, but I still must realize that I may be forever impaired. The Garfield incident teaches me about us prodigal people…We have come home, but continue to growl and limp with our woundings. The Father's love can't quite ease the pig bite scrars, force our brothers to love us, or make our toes grow back.

    In the midst of the celebration there is weeping for "What Might Have Been…" We are forever changed, but should be full of hope because we do have the Father's love and we've had enough sense to come home!

# The Garden of Even
A prayer of thanks for "God's perfect faithfulness"

EVEN after Adam, Eve, and I were thrust from the Garden,
your perfectly faithful Father-love could not be extinguished.
It burned brighter than the sword of the angelic guard
at the eastern gate.

EVEN though exile was appropriate, your Father's heart
grieved at our loss of Paradise
and tender friendship with you.

EVEN while undeserved, my tiny garden mirrors the splendor of yours,
"She that hath eyes to see, has seen…"
Chrome-yellow finches
Scarlet cardinals
Jays of startling blue
Tail-waving squirrels: black, gray, brown
Daisies and dahlias and sweet peas, oh, my
Catnip and peppermint, and

# MORNING GLORY AIRPORT

Purple blossomed butterfly bush…
Amazing.

EVEN when you show your spectacular grandeur in miniature,
framed by mykitchen window,
I quiver in awe of what might have been…

There is a tree, but it cannot share knowledge of good and evil.
It simply houses many happy squirrel families.
Birds nest, cradled in its branches.

My Tigris and Euphrates birdbath sits central
offering a place to bathe and drink—
and for me –a spot to think.

EVEN now—most important of all…
Your remedy for sin is made visible:
A seed is planted.
It is dead in the earth,
But then bursts forth from ground's grave—
**NEW LIFE**
Resurrection! Restoration! Reconciliation!

THANK YOU for your perfect faithfulness.

"O Lord, you are my God, I will exalt you and praise your name, for in perfect faithfulness you have done marvelous things, things planned long ago." Isaiah 25:1

# The Secret

And still another garden—
Robin peaks around the corner.
Daffodil hesitantly pokes through the dark sod.
Spring is whispering a secret:
"The world is coming back to life."

Meanwhile I am trudging through Lent,
Pretending to sacrifice what really isn't mine
So I can meditate/contemplate.

I know a secret too.
With it comes a journey to Jerusalem.

Palms and joyous merriment. Palm Sunday.

Communion with Christ and His disciples.
It is Maundy Thursday. (I am begging to be spared the role of Judas.)

## MORNING GLORY AIRPORT

But we move on to Good Friday. We grieve in silent darkness.
Christ has been crucified; He is dead!
Dear friends prepare His body and bury him.
We wait.

We join the ones inquiring in the garden.
THEN the magnificent secret is revealed:

The tomb is empty!
Christ is risen. He is risen indeed. It is Easter.
And in harmony with Spring and its new life,
We sing, even with tears of joy.
Our voices echo over the hillside:

"Christ the Lord is risen today."
HAL-LE-LU-JAH!

Easter season, 2022

# The Eight Who Ate

There were eight deer this morning.
I watched them graze
Across the back yard
In their winsome ways.

"How 'bout a lily leaf?"
Said one to another.
"I'm eating hosta,"
Came the voice from his brother.

Three spotted babies
Were learning the drill.
I should have been angry
And someday I will

Shoo them away,
Just not today.
In fact, I'll enjoy them
as long as they stay.

August 18, 2020

# Hummingbird Feeder

The hummingbird feeder is empty.
There's a touch of chill in the air.
I am sad at my kitchen window
To see the clear feeder out there.

In summer the hovering beauties
Buzzed about, draining each yellow cup.
Their bodies shimmered with color
So I kept on filling them up.

I love my hovering flyers
Who trust me to sweeten the brew.
But winter soon will be coming,
So the most loving thing to do…

No longer supply the red nectar
Which hung for my friends from the tree.

## NANCY CORBETT

Bid a fond farewell for their journey,
And hope they come back to me.

When the winter has finally ended,
As it always has before,
I'll pour the lush, red nectar
To hang near the kitchen door.

Then my sparkling, flittering wee ones
Will wave and drink their fill.
And JOY will return to the kitchen
From over the window sill.

Late summer, 1998

# Gracie

Imagine "one cup of cat." That was Gracie! She weighed eight ounces when she became our cat. What a tiny, desperate kitty. It all began when I had just stepped in the door from work at Zane State, where I taught. Bob said, "Keep your coat on we have to go to the vet."

My comment: "Oh, no, who's sick?" At the time the place was crowded with cats Puff, Mary Catherine, and Patrick (a sister/brother team we had gotten at Tractor Supply). Oh, they weren't on sale, but a farmer had brought in the two barn cats in hopes of finding them a home. Bob had gone there to get some boxes because we were moving. I think he did get the boxes, but in one he also brought the homeless pair. We also had three dogs at the time. What a crazy household. Six pets! So I feared one had "taken ill." Not so.

Bob told his story: "I was driving along on Olde Falls Road on my way to buy paint." (He owns and operates a cabinet shop in our town.) "Just in front of me I saw a splotch of black and white on the road. I thought it might be a baby skunk, but I didn't have the heart to run over it. I put on my flashers to warn the on-coming driver that I was stopping and he waited as I scooped her up. It found it was a tiny kitten." As the story progressed, he explained he had gone to several houses to see if she belonged to anyone, but she must have been a forgotten part of a litter whose members had simply moved on. The negligent mother must not have missed the runt.

The vet held out little hope that the tiny patient would survive. She was emaciated and he wasn't sure she had eyes, since the eyelids were matted completely shut." Here we go again," I thought.

It was like a winter re-run of previous cat adoptions like Willie and Puff and other strays. We really couldn't afford the care, but didn't want her to die. Several days and many dollars later, we took her home. By then we had named her Grace, after Bob's mother.

As it all unfolded, Puff grudgingly adopted her. Puff was getting up in years, eventually dying at age 22. Meanwhile she was Gracie's surrogate mother. Gracie began to thrive. She wedged her way into the pet system and provided entertainment because she still liked to play as the youngest family member. She enjoyed batting the water in the dog's bowl and spread water everywhere around it. We questioned if she might have been a fish in a previous life, but really didn't believe in reincarnation.

She once hid herself in the rafters of the historic, unfinished house we were remodeling. When we finally did find her, she was covered in coal dust from previous generations. It took several baths under protest to re-discover her beautiful long white fur. We didn't attempt to wash away her original black trim.

Today we've settled into a home without dirty rafters. She happily scuffles with Mary Catherine and once in a while starts out her nights in my bed where Mary Catherine often sleeps. I enjoy Gracie's visits, but find she leaves me when I turn out the light. I miss her when she goes, often catapulting to a high window sill where she spies on the neighbors. In the day time she follows me to the basement and waits as I do laundry, but that's also the spot where they eat and have their litter. Best of all, it's a wide open area and, when she's in the mood, I kick ping pong balls across the floor for her to chase. It's a fun diversion from the day's routine. Right now she's draped over the back of the couch looking out the window with hopes the neighbor's patchwork cat will drop by.

I tend to live a metaphorical life, seeing our pets as they relate to me as their "god-figure" and my behavior as I relate to the real God. Like Gracie, I too have been redeemed and restored. I watch for colorful spots in daily life like imagining a morning glory airport or seeing the lives of our pets as memorable. I feel deeply loved and valued. The real God makes that sense of well being available to all if we only recognize and accept the gift.

# About the Author

Nancy Corbett is a life-long resident of Zanesville, a small town in Southeastern Ohio. She earned her Bachelors of Arts in English at Nyack College in Nyack, New York; her Masters in Interpersonal Communication form Ohio University. With a variety of job experiences, including hospital public relations director, radio station "stringer," TV weather girl, and children's show host she discovered—at last—that her true calling was teaching. She worked for thirty-nine years at Philo High School; then after retirement, she taught for ten more years as an adjunct instructor in communications at Zane State College but has now re-retired.

She is married to Bob, and in their blended family there are six adult children. Presently as an active member of Trinity Evangelical Lutheran Church in Zanesville, she feels she is a contented follower of the Good Shepherd and is waiting with enthusiasm to learn what new opportunities will be available now that she is "out to pasture."

www.ingramcontent.com/pod-product-compliance
Lightning Source LLC
LaVergne TN
LVHW010308070426
835510LV00025B/3415